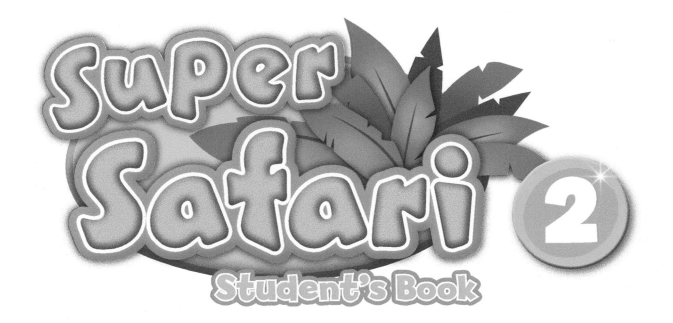

Super Safari 2

Student's Book

Herbert Puchta   **Günter Gerngross**   **Peter Lewis-Jones**

CAMBRIDGE
UNIVERSITY PRESS

Map of the book

Hello! (pages 4–7)

Vocabulary	Chant: Grammar
Mike, Gina, Polly, Leo	What's your name? I'm …

▶ Total physical response: Say "hello!"   Smile   Shake hands   High five | **▶ Song: Hello!**

1 My school (pages 8–15)

Vocabulary	Chant: Grammar	Story and value	CLIL	Thinking skills
board, paper, computer, desk, crayon, pencil case	This is my (crayon).	*The medals* Appreciating differences	Move your body	Sorting

▶ Total physical response: Open your book   Pick up your crayon   Draw a picture   Oh, no! It's broken! | **▶ Song: I have a pencil case on my desk**

2 My body (pages 16–23)

Vocabulary	Chant: Grammar	Story and value	CLIL	Thinking skills
arms, hands, feet, legs, body, head	I can (clap my hands).	*Ouch!* Taking care of someone	Animal bodies	Noticing details

▶ Total physical response: Kick a ball   It's a goal   Clap your hands   Hug your friend | **▶ Song: Shake your body!**

3 My room (pages 24–31)

Vocabulary	Chant: Grammar	Story and value	CLIL	Thinking skills
toy box, bookcase, lamp, rug, window, door	Where's my (book)? It's in / on / under the (bookcase).	*Good night, Dad* Being patient	Cleaning up	Comparing

▶ Total physical response: Where's my rabbit?   Look under the rug   Look in the toy box   Ah, here it is | **▶ Song: My messy room**

4 In the jungle (pages 32–39)

Vocabulary	Chant: Grammar	Story and value	CLIL	Thinking skills
rhino, tiger, elephant, snake, spider, crocodile	Is it a (rabbit)? Yes, it is. / No, it isn't.	*The jungle* Being creative	Where animals live	Noticing details

▶ Total physical response: Walk through the jungle   Turn around   It's a big snake   Run away! | **▶ Song: Walking through the jungle**

5 Fruits and vegetables (pages 40–47)

Vocabulary	Chant: Grammar	Story and value	CLIL	Thinking skills
potatoes, pineapple, carrots, tomatoes, watermelon, banana	Do you like (vegetables)? Yes, I do. / No, I don't.	*The fruit salad* Healthy eating	Food types	Comparing, contrasting

▶ **Total physical response:** Hmm … I'm hungry   Look, there's an apple   I can't reach   Jump … Ouch! ▶ **Song: Do you like vegetables?**

6 My town (pages 48–55)

Vocabulary	Chant: Grammar	Story and value	CLIL	Thinking skills
bus stop, park, school, toy store, supermarket, zoo	Let's go to (the park).	*The present* Keeping your town clean	The environment	Creating associations

▶ **Total physical response:** It's a toy store … wow   What's this?   Look … a robot.   Oh, no! ▶ **Song: Come and see my town!**

7 Jobs (pages 56–63)

Vocabulary	Chant: Grammar	Story and value	CLIL	Thinking skills
farmer, police officer, builder, doctor, firefighter, teacher	My (mom)'s a (doctor).	*Firefighters* Helping others	Jobs and vehicles	Sorting

▶ **Total physical response:** I'm a farmer   Listen … what's that?   It's a bull! Run! ▶ **Song: Let's play firefighters!**

8 The weather (pages 64–71)

Vocabulary	Chant: Grammar	Story and value	CLIL	Thinking skills
rainy, windy, cold, snowy, hot, sunny	Is it (hot / cold / sunny / snowy)? Yes, it is. / No, it isn't.	*The island* Being prepared	Weather and geography	Sequencing

▶ **Total physical response:** It's a hot and sunny day … phew   Put your hat on   Eat ice cream … yum   Oh, no, the sea! Run! ▶ **Song: What's the weather like today?**

9 In the country (pages 72–79)

Vocabulary	Chant: Grammar	Story and value	CLIL	Thinking skills
tree, leaves, frog, grass, flower, bee	The bee is / isn't (big). It's (small).	*The bee* Respecting nature	Animal habitats	Sorting

▶ **Total physical response:** I'm walking in the yard   Look, it's a flower   Look, it's a bird   Ouch! It's a tree! ▶ **Song: Four frogs on a tree**

Phonics (pages 80–89)

Unit 1:	Unit 2:	Unit 3:	Unit 4:	Unit 5:	Unit 6:	Unit 7:	Unit 8:	Unit 9:	Phonics
"a" cat, dad	"i" sit, pin	"e" bed, pen	"o" dot, pot	"u" cut, bus	"m" mom, map	"j" jam, job	"l" log, lamp	"w" wet, wow	review

Review **pages 90–94**   **Certificate:** 95   **Stickers:** End section

 www.cambridge.org/supersafari/familyfun   3

Hello!

CD1 02 **Listen and point. Say the names.**

1 Mike 2 Gina 3 Polly 4 Leo

2 CD1 03 **Listen and chant.**

1

2

3

4

4 CD1 07 08 **Listen and sing.**

Review → page 90

Family fun!

Singing for fun ⑦

1 My school

1 CD1 09 Listen and point. Say the words.

1 board 2 paper 3 computer 4 desk 5 crayon 6 pencil case

2 CD1 10 Listen and trace. Chant.

1

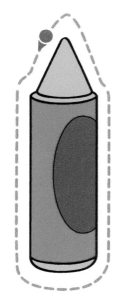

2

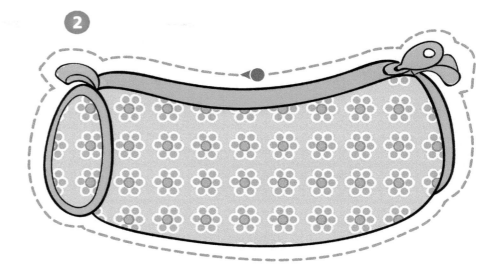

3

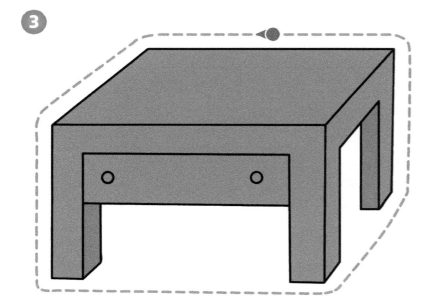

4

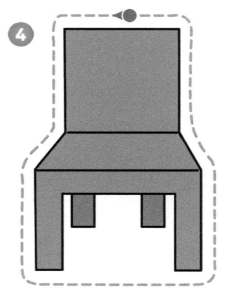

 # Listen and act. Listen and color.

4 CD1 15 16 **Listen and sing.**

The medals

Value: Appreciating differences

Move your body

Listen and point. Trace and say the words.

7 **Think!** **Look and match. Say the actions.**

Thinking skills: Sorting **15**

2 My body

1 arms 2 hands 3 feet 4 legs 5 body 6 head

2 CD1 24 Listen, trace, and match. Chant.

 **3** CD1 26 27 **Listen and act. Listen and color.**

1

2

3

4

4 CD1 29 30 **Listen and sing.**

Ouch!

1

2

3

4

Family fun!

Value: Taking care of someone

Animal bodies

1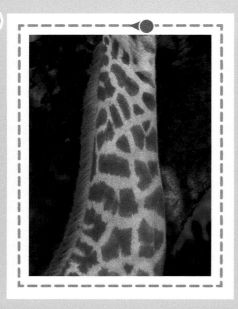

2

3

4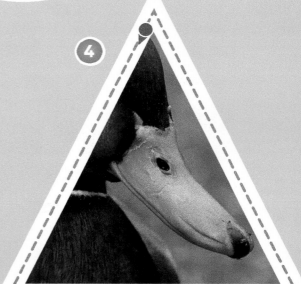

7 (Think!) **Look and match. Say the words.**

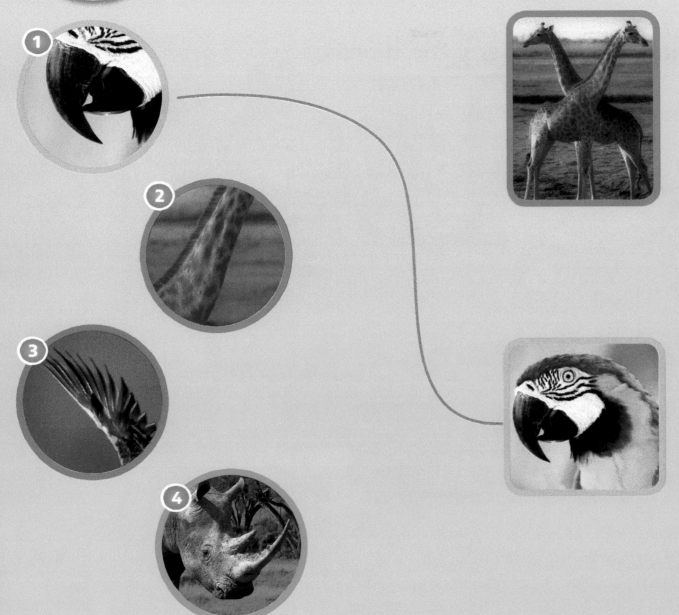

① ② ③ ④

③ My room

24 1 toy box 2 bookcase 3 lamp 4 rug 5 window 6 door

2 CD1 37 **Listen and circle. Chant.**

1

2

Where's my (book)? It's in / on / under the (bookcase).   **25**

3 Listen and act. Listen and color.

CD1 39 40

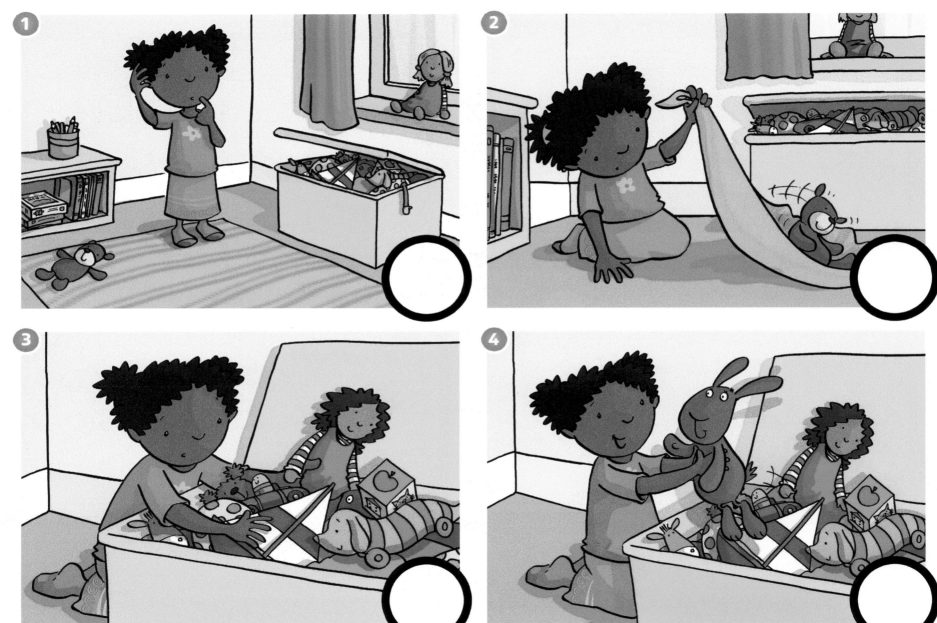

Total physical response

4 CD1 42 43 **Listen and sing.**

Family fun!

Good night, Dad

1

2

3

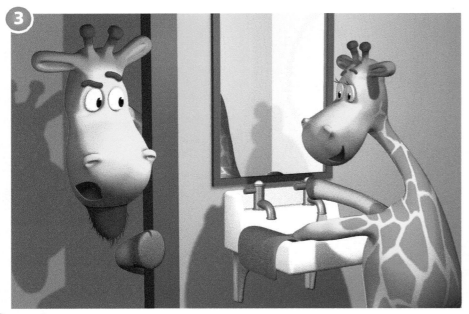

4

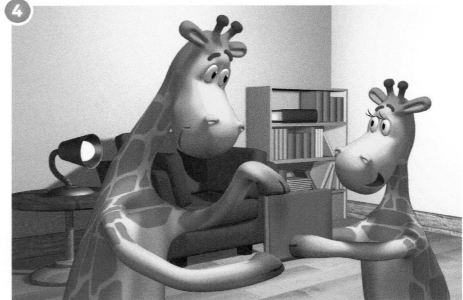

Value: Being patient

Family fun!

Cleaning up

6 CD1 47 **Listen and point. Draw and say the words.**

1

2

7 (Think!) **Find the difference. Circle the objects and say.**

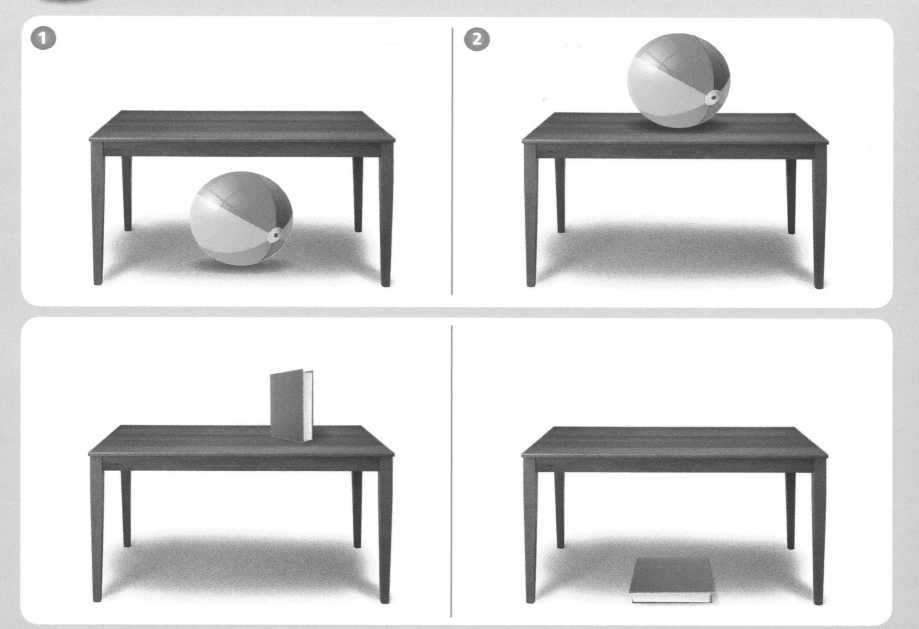

Thinking skills: Comparing   **31**

4 In the jungle

1 CD1 49 **Listen and point. Say the animals.**

1 rhino 2 tiger 3 elephant 4 snake 5 spider 6 crocodile

2 CD1 51 **Listen and trace. Chant.**

 **3** CD1 53 54 **Listen and act. Listen and color.**

1

2

3

4

4 CD1 56 57 **Listen and sing.**

The jungle

Where animals live

 CD1 61

6 Listen and point. Trace and say the animals.

1

2

3

4

7  **Look and circle. What's wrong?**

Thinking skills: Noticing details   39

1 CD1 63 **Listen and point. Say the fruits and vegetables.**

1 potatoes 2 pineapple 3 carrots 4 tomatoes 5 watermelon 6 bananas

2 ^{CD1} 65 **Listen, trace, and color. Chant.**

1

2

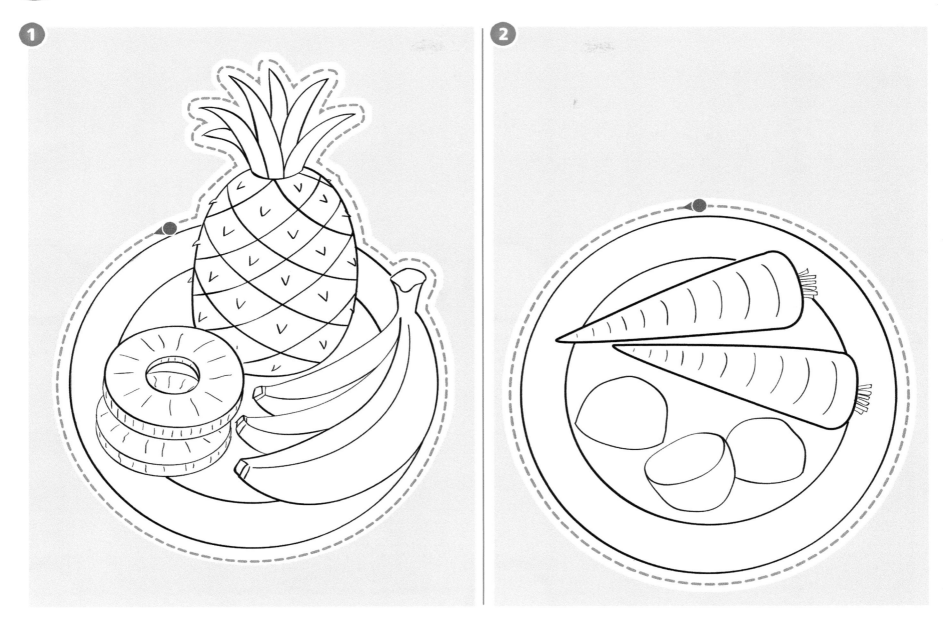

3 Listen and act. Listen and color.

1

2

3

4

4 CD2 04 05 **Listen and sing.**

The fruit salad

Family fun!

Food types

6 CD2 09 **Listen and point. Trace and say the fruits and vegetables.**

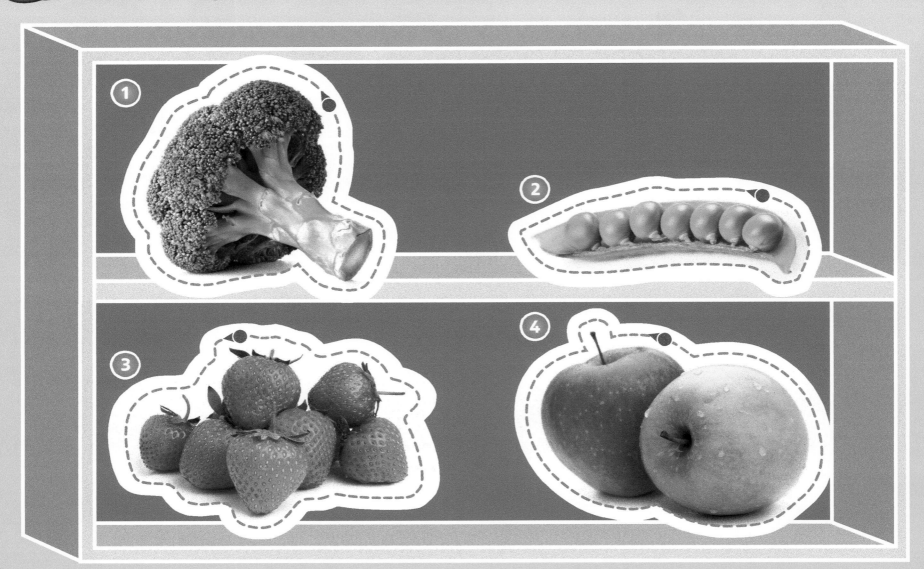

1

2

3

4

7 Think! **Look and circle the fruit.**

1

2

3

4

5

6

Thinking skills: Comparing, contrasting   47

6 My town

1 bus stop 2 park 3 school 4 toy store 5 supermarket 6 zoo

2 CD2 12 Listen and trace. Chant.

 **Listen and act. Listen and color.**

4 CD2 16 17 **Listen and sing.**

6

Family fun!

Singing for fun **51**

The present

1

2

3

4

Family fun!

The environment

6 CD2 21 **Listen and point. Draw and say.**

1

2

7 (Think!) **What's wrong? Look and circle.**

Thinking skills: Creating associations   **55**

7 Jobs

1 farmer 2 police officer 3 builder 4 doctor 5 firefighter 6 teacher

2  **Listen and match. Chant.**

CD2
24

1

2

Family fun!

My (mom)'s a (doctor). 57

4 CD2 29 30 **Listen and sing.**

Firefighters

Jobs and vehicles

6 CD2 34 **Listen and point. Trace and say the words.**

1

2

3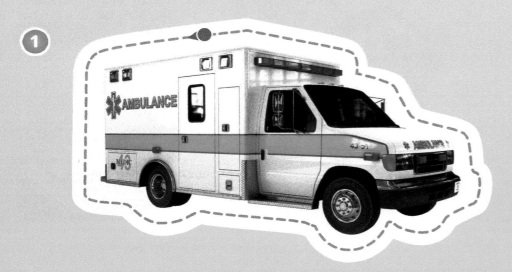

4

7 Think! **Look and match. Say the words.**

①

②

③

④

Thinking skills: Sorting **63**

8 The weather

1 CD2 36 **Listen and point. Say the words.**

64 1 rainy 2 windy 3 cold 4 snowy 5 hot 6 sunny

2 **Listen and match. Chant.**

1

2

1

2

3

4

4 CD2 41 42 **Listen and sing.**

The island

1

2

3

4

Value: Being prepared

Weather and geography

6 CD2 46 **Listen and point. Circle and say the words.**

1

2

7 Think! What's next? Match and say the words.

Phonics → page 87   Review → page 94

9 In the country

72 1 tree 2 leaves 3 frog 4 grass 5 flower 6 bee

2 CD2 49 **Listen and circle. Chant.**

1

2

Listen and act. Listen and color.

1

2

3

4

Total physical response

4 CD2 54 55 **Listen and sing.**

The bee

Value: Respecting nature

Animal habitats

Listen and point. Trace and say the words.

1

2

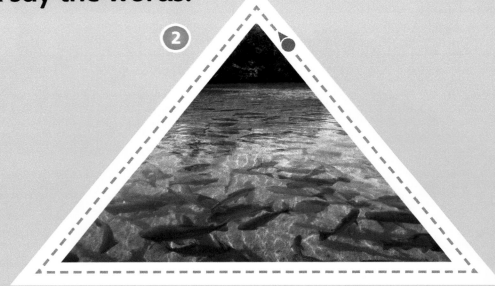

3

4

7 Think! **Look and match. Say the words.**

1

2

3

4

Thinking skills: Sorting   79

1 Look and find.

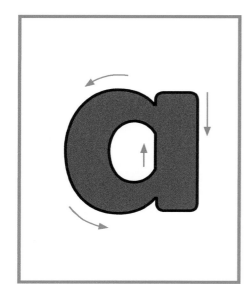

c a t

d a d

2 🖸 CD1 21 Listen and join in.

1 Look and find.

s i t

p i n

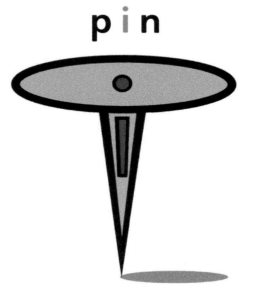

2 Listen and join in.

 **Look and find.**

b e d

p e n

 Listen and join in.

1 Look and find. Color the letter.

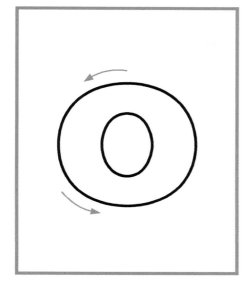

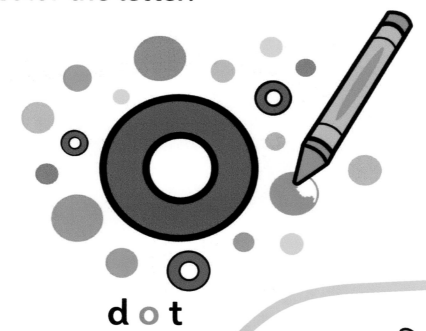

d o t

p o t

2 Listen and join in.

1 Look and find. Color the letter.

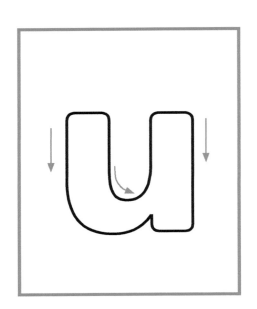

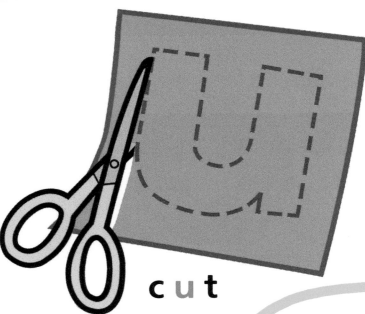

c u t

b u s

1 Look and find. Color the letter.

Phonics

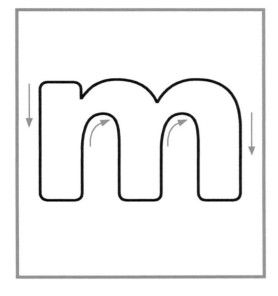

m o m

m a p

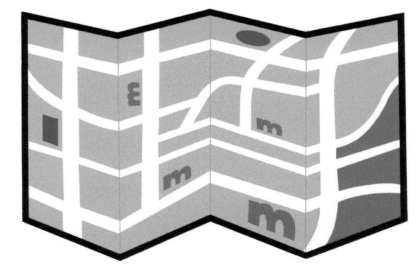

2 CD2 22 Listen and join in.

1 Look and find. Trace the letter.

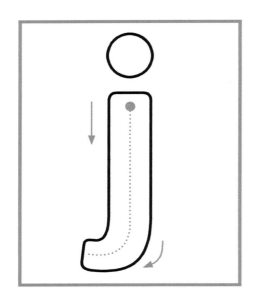

j a m

j o b

2 Listen and join in.

1 **Look and find. Trace the letter.**

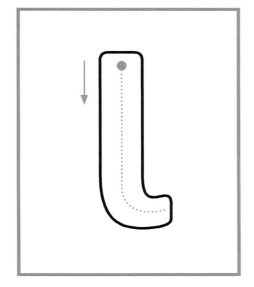

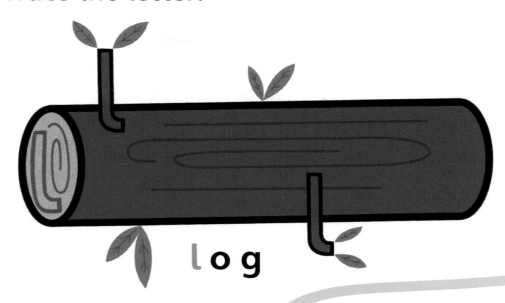

l o g

l a m p

2 **Listen and join in.**

1 Look and find. Trace the letter.

w e t

w o w

2 🎵 CD2 60 Listen and join in.

j a m

l a m p

w e t

p o t

m a p

b u s

c a t

p i n

p e n

1 Listen to the sentences. Color the frames.

1 CD2 63 **Listen and color the circles. Color the frames.**

CD2 64 **Listen and color the circles. Color the frames.**

1 Listen and color the circles. Color the frames.

1 [CD2 66] Listen and color the circles. Color the frames.

Good job!

....

has finished Super Safari!

Thanks and acknowledgments

Authors' thanks

The authors would like to thank a number of people who have made significant contributions towards the final form of Super Safari: Colin Sage, Helen Brock, and Carolyn Wright, our editors, for their expertise in working on the manuscripts, and the support we got from them.

Our designers, Blooberry, for their imaginative layout and all the artists – in particular Bill Bolton – for the inspiring artwork that has brought our ideas to life in such beautiful ways.

Liane Grainger, Managing Editor and Emily Hird, Publisher, for their many useful suggestions for improvement.

Jason Mann, Editorial Director at Cambridge University Press, for his vision and encouragement.

The publishers are grateful to the following contributors:

Blooberry Design: cover design, book design, publishing management, and page make-up
Bill Bolton: cover illustration
Alison Prior: picture research
John Marshall Media: audio recording and production
James Richardson: chant writing and production
Robert Lee, Dib Dib Dub Studios: song writing and production
Lisa Hutchins: freelance editor

The publishers and authors are grateful to the following illustrators:

Bill Bolton; Judy Brown; Gareth Conway (The Bright Agency); Kate Daubney; Mark Duffin; Louise Garner; Sue King (Plum Pudding Illustration); Bernice Lum

The authors and publishers acknowledge the following sources of copyright material and are grateful for the permissions granted. While every effort has been made, it has not always been possible to identify the sources of all the material used, or to trace all copyright holders. If any omissions are brought to our notice, we will be happy to include the appropriate acknowledgments on reprinting.

The publishers are grateful to the following for permission to reproduce copyright photographs and material:

p.14 (L): Alamy/© Rubberball; p.14 (TR): Superstock/© Rubberball; p.14 (BL): Alamy/© Picture Partners; p.14 (BR): Shutterstock/© Maria Mykhaliuk; p.15 (TC): Shutterstock/© Stuart Monk; p.15 (TR): Shutterstock/© Dmitri Maruta; p.15 (BC): Shutterstock/© Andresr; p.15 (BR): Shutterstock/© Natalia Matreeva; p.15 (BL): Shutterstock/© Ksenia Tupitsyna; p.15 (C): Shutterstock/© Andresr; p.15 (TL): Shutterstock/© Glenda; p.22 (TL): Shutterstock/© Sharon Haegar; p.22 (TR): Shutterstock/© apiguide; p.22 (BC): Shutterstock/© Panu Ruangian; p.22 (BR): Shutterstock/© Sh.el.Photo; p.23 (TC & 2): Shutterstock/© Pearl Media; p.23 (BR & 4): Shutterstock/© Volodymr Burdiak; p.23 (TR & 3): Shutterstock/© John Michael Evan Potter;p.23 (BC & I): Shutterstock/© Dmitrijs Mihejevs; p.30 (L): Corbis/© Jo-Ann Richards/ First Light; p.30 (R): Getty Images/© Andrew Hetherington; p.31 (table): Shutterstock/© Horiyan; p.31 (ball): Shutterstock/© Mejnak; p.31 (book): Shutterstock/© StudioVin; p.38 (TL): Shutterstock/© Peter Wollinga; p.38 (TR): Shutterstock/© Andrew Burgess; p.38 (BR): Shutterstock/© Kamonrat; p.38 (BL): Shutterstock/© Praisaeng; p.46 (TL): Shutterstock/© gilmar; p.46 (TR): Shutterstock/© Mazzur/ p.46 (BL): Shutterstock/© Aleksey Troshin; p.46 (BR): Shutterstock/© Petr Malyshev; p.47 (TL): Shutterstock/© Jiri Hera; p.47 (TC): Shutterstock/© Dionisvera; p.47 (TR): Shutterstock/© Aleksey Troshin; p.47 (BL): Shutterstock/© Betacam-SP; p.47 (BC): Shutterstock/© ravl; p.47 (BR): Shutterstock/© EM Arts; p.54 (L): Shutterstock/© WDG Photo; p.54 (R): Alamy/© Gruffydd; p.62 (TL): Alamy/© Kumar Sriskandan; p.62 (TR): Shutterstock/© Bjorn Heller; p.62 (BL): Shutterstock/© Tyler Olson; p.62 (BR): Shutterstock/© Digital Storm; p.63 (I): Alamy/© eye35; p.63 (2): Shutterstock/© Tupungato; p.63 (3) Alamy/© Kumar Sriskandan; p.63 (4) Shutterstock/© Ben Carlson; p.63 (TL): Corbis/© 237/Chris Ryan/ Ocean; p.63 (TR): Shutterstock/© John Roman Images; p.63 (BL): Alamy/© Cultura Creative; p.63 (BR): Shutterstock/© Bonita R. Cheshier; p.70 (L): Shutterstock/© Volodymer Goink; p.70 (R): Shutterstock/© Microstock Man; p.78 (TL): Shutterstock/© Micha Klootwijk; p.78 (TR): Shutterstock/© Christian Kohler; p.78 (BL): Frank Lane Picture Agency/© Bill Coster; p.78 (BR): Shutterstock/© Alexey Stiop; p.79 (I) Shutterstock/© Hintau Alaksei; p.79 (2): Shutterstock/© Panbazil; p.79 (3): Shutterstock/© Irinak; p.79 (4): Shutterstock/© Jang Hongyan; p.79 (T): Shutterstock/© Ron Zmiri; p.79 (CR): Shutterstock/© M Pellinni; p.79 (CL): Shutterstock/© Konstantnin; p.79 (BR): Shutterstock/© pzAxe.

page 53

page 61

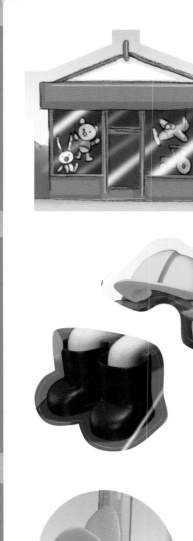

UNIT 8
page 69

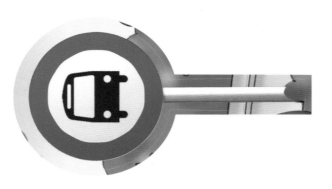

FUN STICKERS

page 77

pages 90–94